# Writing
# High-Impact Reports:
Proven Practices for
Auditors and Accountants

**By Angela J. Maniak**

**Skill-Builders Press**
Northport, Maine

**If you would like additional copies of the book or CD-ROM, please contact:**
**Angela J. Maniak**
**207-338-0108**
**www.angelamaniak.com**

# Writing High-Impact Reports:
Proven Practices for Auditors and Accountants

**Dear readers,**

In this book, you will discover how you can influence readers and show the value of your work through your written communication. You will learn how to write reports that:

- Communicate issues concisely and concretely.
- Convey impacts convincingly.
- Document action plans that produce benefits and reduce risks.

*Writing High-Impact Reports* shows you how to write it right the first time, thus avoiding costly edits and rewrites. I take the unique approach of focusing on **what you need to do before writing a report.** I lay out a step-by-step process you can use to:

- Compose a good first draft quickly.
- Communicate your message directly, persuasively, and simply.
- Minimize rewriting by self or others.
- Publish timely reports.

The instructions, examples, and exercises are uniquely customized for audit and accounting professionals, making the materials relevant, practical, and immediately useful. In this book, I share the proven techniques I have taught in audit report-writing workshops for 20 years.

Regards,

*Angela J. Maniak*

**Writing High-Impact Reports:**
Proven Practices for Auditors and Accountants

# Table of Contents

# Notes

# Notes

# Notes

**Writing High-Impact Reports:**
Proven Practices for Auditors and Accountants

By Angela J. Maniak

# Why You Need This Book to Succeed in Your Profession

Your clients rely on you—an audit or financial professional—to provide them with critical business information they need to manage their work successfully. Your clients—individuals, groups, organizations, or corporations—depend on you to help decipher the meaning of numbers, recommend appropriate accounting methods, analyze controls or operating systems, or conclude on the correctness of information. In short, they rely on you to help them and their businesses save, make, or manage money.

The way you help your clients succeed is by offering them the information they need, in a form and style they can use and act on. Most often, clients need and want this information in writing. They may need to decide actions on the basis of your report, distribute your results to other individuals or groups, keep a historical record, or even fulfill regulatory or legal requirements. Clients depend on your written communications to help them achieve these goals.

The reports you write must meet your readers' particular needs. They must be:
- Compact and easy to read.
- Understandable to a broad, often non-financial, audience.
- Compelling and persuasive.

To meet such needs, you cannot simply present the detailed data that results from the research and analysis you do. You must condense, consolidate, and prioritize your points. You must present your conclusions and recommendations in a written form that is easy to understand and act upon. Therefore, as an accounting, auditing, or financial professional, you are likely to spend much of your working life writing reports. Unfortunately, writing may not be your favorite part of the job.

**How do *you* feel about writing on the job?**

Maybe you don't *mind* writing, you'd just rather spend your time *doing other things.*

Maybe you *do* mind writing, and you put it off as long as possible, until a deadline is staring you straight in the face.

Maybe you're *not very confident* of your writing skills—after all, it's been a few years since your last English course.

Maybe you think you *write just fine,* but your boss or colleagues like to have a field day editing or rewriting your perfectly acceptable prose.

Wherever you see yourself in these scenarios, you are a professional writer. Your clients, bosses, and colleagues expect you to create and deliver a product, and that product is a report of your professional results—data, opinions, analyses, recommendations. In your written reports, you need to **tell your clients what they need to know, in a way they can understand it, and in a manner that enables them to act.**

## Your Payback from Using This Book

The goal of my book is to enable you to write it right the first time. I take the unique approach of focusing on **what you need to do before writing a report.** Following the step-by-step process I recommend will make composition and self-review faster and will enable you to:

- Write more quickly.
- Publish timely reports.
- Minimize rewriting by self or others.

This book will teach you to present your results clearly, concretely, convincingly, and concisely. It will show you how to avoid costly edits and rewrites. You will learn to compose efficiently, review your own writing thoroughly, and produce polished, professional reports. You will also understand how to determine what your readers expect of your documents and—even more important—how to display the value of your work through your written communication.

## Who Will Benefit from This Book

This book is uniquely customized for accounting, audit, and financial professionals. Those who will benefit most include:

- Accounting managers and directors
- Business analysts
- Compliance auditors
- Credit analysts
- Environmental auditors
- Financial analysts
- Government auditors
- Internal auditors
- Internal-control specialists
- Loan reviewers
- Public accountants
- Quality-control specialists
- Tax professionals

Ultimately, your clients will be the key beneficiaries of this book, as they profit from your clear, concise, useful reports.

## What This Book Will Teach You to Write

This book focuses on narrative reports that provide analysis, conclusions, or recommendations. Examples of such reports include:

- Compliance review
- Consultation report
- Internal audit report
- Internal control analysis
- Loan review report
- Management letter
- Operational review
- Quality audit
- Regulatory reviews

## Bonus Material Is Included

The CD-ROM included with this book provides you with a portable resource you can carry with you. This is especially helpful if you travel for your work and want to lighten your load by leaving the book on your desk. The CD contains:

- Key points of each chapter
- Printable writing tips and worksheets
- Answers to exercises in the book
- A sample report illustrating the concepts explained in the book
- Review excercise for each chapter

The book also contains a laminated Tip Sheet that documents the step-by-step writing process and includes key points for completing each writing step. You can tuck this into your briefcase or post it near your computer screen.

# How to Write It Right the First Time:

**A Step-by-Step Process**

**Before You Compose:**

- Start with a Written Objective.
- Design an Assembly Process for Report Writing.
- Document and Communicate Issues Promptly, Using the 5 Cs as a Writing Tool.
- Decide on the Organization and Format of the Report.

**As You Compose:**

- Get to the Point.
- Sell Key Points.
- Get Commitment to Key Points.

**After You Compose:**

- Fine-Tune Your Report: Review for Conciseness and Correctness.

# How to Write It Right the First Time:
## A Step-by-Step Process

**1**

**Before You Compose**

**Write Objectives**

**Write Comment Worksheets**

**Decide on Format**

---

**2**

**As You Compose**

**Write Draft Report**

- Get to the Point
- Sell Key Points
- Get Commitment

---

**3**

**After You Compose**

**Review for Conciseness**

**Proofread for Correctness**

**Issue Final Report**

# Proven Writing Techniques Eliminate Common Report-Writing Weaknesses

| Report Weakness to Avoid | Writing Technique to Use | Where to Find It |
|---|---|---|
| Unfocused: Hard to Find the Key Message | ■ Put the Objective in Writing When You Begin a Project | Chapter 1 |
| Incomplete Support for Issues Presented | ■ Use the 5 Cs to Develop and Document Comments | Chapter 2 |
| Weak Introduction: Report Does Not Get to the Point Quickly | ■ Structure the Report for Greatest Impact ■ Layer the Report for Multiple Audiences | Chapter 3 |
| Report Is Not Easily Legible and It Is Hard to Find Information | ■ Format for Readability ■ Write a Summary | Chapter 3 |
| Points are Ambiguous or Hard to Understand | ■ Keep It Concrete ■ Write in Simple Business Terms | Chapter 4 |
| Too Much Background Information | ■ Start Each Section with the Key Point | Chapter 4 |

## Proven Writing Techniques Eliminate Common Report-Writing Weaknesses

| Report Weakness to Avoid | Writing Technique to Use | Where to Find It |
|---|---|---|
| Evidence Is Insufficient to Persuade Readers or There Is Too Much Detail | ■ Offer Factual Evidence | Chapter 5 |
| Significance of Issues Is Not Clear or Perspective is Lacking | ■ Show Consequences from the Reader's Viewpoint<br>■ Describe or Quantify the Impact of Issues | Chapter 5 |
| Tone is Critical, Judgmental, or Unbalanced | ■ Avoid Overstating or Understating the Significance<br>■ Confront Likely Objections | Chapter 5 |
| Recommendations are Weak or Nonexistent | ■ Write Recommendations that Fix and Prevent Problems<br>■ Focus on the Cause | Chapter 6 |

## Proven Writing Techniques Eliminate Common Report-Writing Weaknesses

| Report Weakness to Avoid | Writing Technique to Use | Where to Find It |
|---|---|---|
| Accountability for Solutions is Lacking | ■ Document Action Plans that Establish Accountability | Chapter 6 |
| Recommendations Appear Trivial or Not Cost-Effective | ■ Write Practical Recommendations<br>■ Describe the Benefits of Action Plans | Chapter 6 |
| Report is Wordy or Too Lengthy | ■ Say What You Mean in as Few Words as Possible | Chapter 7 |
| Sentences are Hard to Understand | ■ Bias Your Writing Toward the Active Voice | Chapter 7 |
| Report Contains Grammatical or Punctuation Errors | ■ Don't Let Mistakes Slip By: Perform a Self-Edit | Chapter 8 |

## Notes

CHAPTER 1

 # Start Every Project with an Objective

**Key Points**

⇄  Make Your Writing Objective-Driven and Value-Added

⇄  Put the Objective in Writing When You Begin a Project

⇄  Avoid Generalizations

⇄  State the Objective in Concrete and Measurable Terms

⇄  Keep It Brief, Even If You Have Multiple Objectives

## Notes

CHAPTER 1
# Start Every Project with an Objective

## Make Your Writing Objective-Driven and Value-Added

A frequent fatal flaw of business writing is the inability of writers to articulate clearly what they want to say. The writers may have written many pages, put many hours into a document, and even edited their writing carefully, but these writers do not have a clear message to communicate.

Often, I have read through a five- or ten-page report, looked up at the author, and asked: "What are you trying to say?" Usually the author rambles on in response, and I listen attentively, and I finally have to ask questions such as: "Why did you write this report?" or "What was the purpose of the project you did?" When the author still struggles to answer my question, I know we are facing a difficult rewrite.

You can save yourself the time and agony of rewriting reports if you discipline yourself to start every project, and certainly every document you write, with a clear understanding of the objective. Many rambling reports might not have been written at all if the writers had been required to state clear, concrete, measurable objectives for the documents before writing them.

On the other hand, other documents are focused, useful, clear and — ultimately—long-lived. Clients value these focused documents, act on them, keep them, and refer to them again in the future. They may share them with colleagues or even try to copy their format or style simply because they find these documents so easy to read and use.

These effective documents provide value and live long lives because they are written to answer specific objectives, not just present information. Let's take a look at how you can ensure that your writing will be objective-driven and value-added.

## Put the Objective in Writing When You Begin a Project

If every document has a purpose, then every work project has a clear objective. When you start an audit or consulting engagement, or any other type of analytical project, you should know and be able to state the desired outcome of that project. What specific need are you meeting for a client? What specific questions do you intend to answer?

### Examples of Objectives:

For instance, if you are reviewing quarterly financial information, perhaps the **objectives** are to:

> **Verify the completeness and accuracy of reported financial results and determine whether the results are reported in compliance with Generally Accepted Accounting Principles.**

If you are evaluating the controls in an accounts payable process, perhaps the objectives are to:

> **Determine if payments made to customers were accurate, timely, and authorized by an approved contract or purchase order.**

If your project is to assess regulatory compliance, the objectives might be to:

> **Determine whether the company identified all applicable laws and regulations, designed and implemented procedures to comply with those laws and regulations, and has an ongoing process to monitor and report on compliance.**

**Writing Tip # 1:**
**How to Write an Objective**

An objective will always include **WHAT** you are reviewing **(accounts payable)** and **WHY** you are reviewing **(to determine if payments made to customers were accurate, timely, and authorized by an approved contract or purchase order).**

To write an objective, consider: "What specific questions does the reader of my report want answered?"

## Avoid Generalizations

Avoid the temptation to state your objective in general or vague terms, such as *"review the quarterly financial results," "evaluate controls over accounts payable,"* or *"review regulatory compliance."* Each of these statements leaves unanswered the question WHY. The objective must describe the reason for and not just the topic of the review.

Even adding a descriptive word is not enough. Consider the following.

**Examples of Vague Objectives:**

**The purpose was to review the adequacy of controls.**

**The objective was to evaluate the reasonableness of financial information.**

**The purpose was to assess the effectiveness of the regulatory function.**

Each of these vague objectives will lead to a vague and disjointed or unfocused report. They are broad statements, and the writer is likely to include too much detail on the subject rather than focusing on a few key points that interest the readers. Even worse, the sample objectives are likely to create a judgmental report that readers do not take seriously. How does one define the *"adequacy"* of controls? What determines whether a number is *"reasonable"* or not? And who is to say whether a function is *"effective"?* What standards or measures are being used to draw conclusions?

## State the Objective in Concrete and Measurable Terms

When you write the objective, think about how you will determine your own answer to that objective. Consider what factual evidence you will use to make up your mind. Identify the precise criteria you will use to draw conclusions. This thinking process will help you write objectives in concrete and measurable terms.

Let's start with a personal example. You may decide that a personal objective is to *"improve my eating habits."* How will you measure your success against the goal? Is any change you make in your diet an *"improvement"*? And what or whose criteria are you using? Is it your own judgment or the guidelines of an authoritative source?

To make the objective measurable, you might state: ***"Lose 15 pounds and keep it off for six months."*** Or, you may say: ***"Cut my meat consumption by 50 percent and substitute fresh vegetables and whole grains."***

Applying this to a business project, consider that you are reviewing the efficiency of a process. Identify what your clients will value most from your report. It won't be enough to tell them that the process is efficient or not efficient (or even "generally efficient"). Neither will it be enough to quantify how long the process takes. Complete Exercise #1 to practice writing concrete and measurable objectives.

## Exercise #1:
## How to Write an Objective

### A) Brainstorm Clients' Questions

Considering the project described (reviewing the efficiency of a process), brainstorm a list of questions you think clients might have. Think about what they will want to see in a final report.

### B) Write the Objectives

Now you are ready to turn the questions into written objectives. Try your hand at this by writing the objectives for this project.

⊙ *Use the CD-ROM to see suggested responses to this exercise.*

## Writing Tip #2:
## How to Write an Objective

Avoid **vague** objectives, such as:

- **Improve the efficiency of the process.**
- **Evaluate the adequacy of controls.**

Write objectives in concrete and measurable terms, such as:

- **Propose methods for reducing labor costs by 10 percent while maintaining current quality and production levels.**
- **Determine whether confidential data is protected from loss, manipulation, or unauthorized access.**

## Keep It Brief, Even If You Have Multiple Objectives

While it is good to be precise in your planning, don't go overboard and get into each and every detail of your project. Auditors and accountants, in the zeal to be logical, thorough, and precise, often write detailed work programs for reviews or testing they perform. These often are written in the concrete and measurable terms that make for good objectives. At the same time, they usually drive down to a level of detail that is inappropriate for a written report to a client.

A recent report I read started with a list of eight objectives. Each one described a specific part of the process that the team reviewed, and each was written in precise and measurable terms. What followed, though, was a list of eight long sentences, each one giving a detailed answer to one of the objectives. The result was choppy and disjointed. As a reader, I could not grasp the overall results of the review or the implications of all the results. The writer was well intentioned and well organized, but forgot to bring the objectives of the review to a higher level—one that his business clients were seeking.

# Writing Tip # 3:
# How to Write an Objective

If your work program or project plan contains numerous objectives or tests, consolidate these into broader themes or categories before you begin the project.

For example, a review of derivative instruments may be planned to include the following tests:

**Determine whether:**
- **Broker accounts were properly approved by the appropriate levels of management.**
- **Broker files were maintained and statements were reconciled.**
- **Hedge worksheets existed for each strategy, contained required information, were properly approved, and were provided timely to Accounting.**
- **Trading activity and open positions were within authorized limits.**
- **Trading and accounting information was presented accurately and completely in internal reports.**
- **Financial entries were properly represented in the general ledger.**

The **project objectives** may be stated in concrete and measurable terms by **consolidating** them as follows:

**The objective of reviewing the derivative instruments was to determine whether:**
- **Broker accounts were approved by an authorized manager.**
- **Brokers maintained required documentation.**
- **Transactions were made within authorized limits.**
- **Transactions were properly recorded in financial records.**

## Notes

CHAPTER 2

 # The 5 Cs: The Writing Tool You Can't Live Without

**Key Points**

⮂ Design an Assembly Process for Report Writing

⮂ Stock Your Writing Toolkit

⮂ Use the 5 Cs to Develop and Document Comments

⮂ Use the 5 Cs to Communicate with Your Client

⮂ Use Comment Worksheets as an Efficient Tool for Report Writing

⮂ Maximize the Quality of Comment Worksheets (And Minimize Future Rewriting of Your Report)

⮂ Write Comment Worksheets Throughout Your Project

## Notes

CHAPTER 2

# The 5 Cs: The Writing Tool You Can't Live Without

## Design an Assembly Process for Report Writing

The most important thing I ever learned about writing is this:

**How you take your notes and organize your research determines how quickly and effectively you can write a report.**

The second most important thing I ever learned about writing is this:

**Don't ever forget the most important thing about writing.**

The bigger the project, the harder it is to write a report. The more information you have to present, the harder it is to decide how to package it. The more people who get involved, the more time it takes to get a document issued. Assembling a business document is akin to assembling any other kind of product. You must have a design, a system, and a process. You must have the right tools. You must know what you want that final product to look like.

As a child, I liked to assemble jigsaw puzzles. I would set up the card table, pour out the 1,000 pieces, prop up the box cover displaying the picture, and get right to work. I would organize the pieces—border pieces first, color groups next, seeking nuances of shading and shadow to get each piece into the right grouping, being wary of false leads, sections that looked alike but were actually far removed in the final piece, or flat sides that really weren't border pieces at all. Before I knew it, the picture was done.

As an adult, I abhor unassembled products. I open the package, pour out the pieces, and look for the instructions and a picture of the final design. The picture on the box rarely resembles the pieces I have taken out of that very same box. The diagram inside, if there is one, looks like something out of a rejected art-school application. The written instructions, when they are included, are in twelve different languages, none of which appears to be my native tongue.

I find the assembly process slow and frustrating, and I forever wonder if I actually got the product together as intended.

Writing can be a lot like this, one way or the other. You can gather all the pieces, then methodically and quickly put them all together. Or you can stare at the pieces, ponder them for hours, keep moving them around and putting them together, only to end up with a bench that wobbles when you stand on it, or wheels that fall off when you push the cart.

Efficient writers know how to manage the process of writing. They find a process that works and stick to it. When working in teams, they share the process with their partners and facilitate the composition of the report. The remainder of this chapter will describe a writing process that can work for you. Use it as presented or modify it to work best for you.

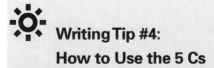

## Writing Tip #4:
## How to Use the 5 Cs

Be an efficient writer by managing the writing process. Design an assembly process before you begin your project.

**How you take your notes and organize your research determines how quickly and effectively you can write a report.**

## Stock Your Writing Toolkit

You can use standard components to build the body of the audit, consultation, or review reports you write. Reports will consist largely of the key conclusions, observations, and issues you want to communicate on your subject. They will usually include recommendations or action steps describing what someone should or will do in response to the issues presented in the report.

An easy and consistent way to keep track of issues and document them as you complete your review is to develop each one using what I call **The 5 Cs.**

### The 5 Cs

For audit, review, and other analytical reports, each issue you present should be developed completely by including the 5 Cs, which enable you to develop your observations to meet the following three purposes of report writing.

| Purpose Achieved | The 5 Cs |
|---|---|
| Inform | Condition Criterion |
| Persuade | Consequence |
| Get Results | Cause Corrective Action |

The tables on pages 26 - 28 describe each of the 5 Cs and give examples

# The 5 Cs:
# The Writing Tool You Can't Live Without

| Component | Description |
|---|---|
| Condition | **Statement of the Issue:** What is the key point you want to communicate to your readers? |
| Criterion | **Description of What Should Be:** What is the policy, standard, principle, or business practice you are evaluating against? |
| Consequence | **Explanation of the Significance or Impact:** What is the impact or materiality? What has gone or could go wrong as a result of the condition? |
| Cause | **Explanation of What Allowed the Condition to Occur:** What is the root cause of the problem? Why was the condition not detected or corrected? |
| Corrective Action | **Description of Action Necessary to Correct the Condition:** What will fix the current condition, and what will prevent it from occurring in the future? |

## The 5 Cs:
## Sample Outline of the 5 Cs

| Component | Example |
|---|---|
| **Condition** | Capital expenditures of $5.8 million for the renovation project were not monitored, and time and budget overruns were not approved. |
| **Criterion** | Finance policy requires continuous monitoring by the project manager and officer approval of capital expenditures over $1 million. |
| **Consequence** | The renovation project was over budget by 25 percent, and the contractors paid no penalties. |
| **Cause** | A project owner had not been appointed to manage the renovation project. |
| **Corrective Action** | The Controller will require a VP's written approval of all capital expenditure project plans, monthly reports, and cost overruns. The VP will appoint a project leader for each capital expenditure project. |

# The 5 Cs:
# Sample Outline of the 5 Cs

| Component | Example |
|---|---|
| **Condition** | Accounts Receivable can reduce past-due balances by billing customers electronically. |
| **Criterion** | Receivables should be collected promptly to maximize cash flow, minimize aging of receivable amounts, and help prevent write-offs. |
| **Consequence** | Electronic invoicing will cut the billing cycle by five days and reduce billing discounts by approximately 3 percent. |
| **Cause** | Accounting systems had to be centralized before electronic billing could be implemented. |
| **Corrective Action** | A project team led by the VP, Accounts Receivables, is working to implement electronic billing by January 31, 200x. |

## Comment Worksheet

**Condition** (Statement of the Issue)

Conclusion: _____

_____

_____

Evidence: _____

_____

_____

**Criterion** (Description of What Should Be) _____

_____

_____

**Consequence** (Significance or Impact) _____

_____

_____

**Cause** (What Allowed the Condition to Occur?) _____

_____

_____

**Corrective Action** (What Will Fix and Prevent the Condition?) _____

Recommendation: _____

_____

_____

Management Action or Response: _____

_____

_____

_____

## Use the 5 Cs to Communicate with Your Clients

The **Comment Worksheet** (an outline of the **5 Cs**) is your most important tool for complete and timely communication and reporting. As you develop conclusions, findings, or recommendations, you need to present them to clients in a logical, complete, and objective fashion. You need to establish clients' agreement to the facts and initiate their buy-in to the need for change. This early presentation and discussion are essential to achieve prompt action on significant items and to ensure the quality and timeliness of the final report.

You may also need to present your results to your own supervisor or manager for review and input. Your manager may want to see evidence of your work and understand the logic of your analysis and conclusions. Comment Worksheets, supported by your workpapers, provide a complete and clear overview of your analytical process.

Finally, issues that you discuss with clients throughout the review will be summarized into a final report. Your Comment Worksheets will form the basis for the body of that report.

### Writing Tip #5:
### How to Use the 5 Cs as a Writing Tool

Write your report as you perform your fieldwork. Document results in a coherent and consistent form, such as the **Comment Worksheet.** At the end of your fieldwork, you will have the body of the report substantially written.

## Use the 5 Cs as a Bridge from Workpapers to Report

The Comment Worksheet helps you make the transition from your detailed workpapers to your condensed final report. Remember your different audiences. Workpapers are intended for your own files only; they are a documentation, not a communication, tool. Reports often go to the highest levels of management within your organization. The form, style, and level of detail of a report may show little connection to the form, style, and level of detail of your workpapers. So how does this magical transformation occur?

It can happen easily through use of the Comment Worksheet. In developing comments, you draw conclusions from your workpapers, and you supplement them with the business analysis (consequence, cause, and corrective action) necessary for successful presentation to management. The business analysis is the most valuable part of your final reports.

## Use Comment Worksheets as an Efficient Tool for Report Writing

Comment Worksheets are an effective tool if you use them at the right time and in the right way.

The **right time** for writing Comment Worksheets is:
- In the field.
- During the review.
- As soon as you identify an issue to communicate to the client or complete a section of work.

The **right way** to use written Comment Worksheets is for:
- Prompt review by your manager.
- Periodic presentations to clients.

**31**

The Comment Worksheet can also incorporate additional administrative information that aids in the review of work and creation of the report. Information you may elect to include consists of items such as:

- Number assigned to the Worksheet
- Cross-reference to workpaper support
- Date
- Name or initials of reviewer
- Disposition
- Cross-reference to report

**Writing Tip #6:**
**How to Use the 5 Cs as a Writing Tool**

**Comment Worksheets help you to:**

- Bridge from workpaper detail to the report.
- Facilitate ongoing discussion of results with client management.
- Allow for interim review of results by management.
- Form the basis for the closing conference and the final report.

## Maximize the Quality of Comment Worksheets (And Minimize Future Rewriting of Your Report)

Comment Worksheets help you to document the results of your work in a structured manner. This in turn encourages you to do a complete and clear analysis of issues before presenting them to clients. The logical organization of your data and ideas helps you determine if your conclusions are complete and convincing.

Here are some tips for writing high quality Comment Worksheets that can form the basis for your report.

### 1. Start with the Criterion.

Even though the criterion is not the first item listed on the Comment Worksheet, it is likely to be the first of the 5 Cs you will document as part of your work plan. Before you begin any review or testing, you must set your criteria. What are you looking for? Why are you conducting these tests? These purposes should always be stated explicitly as objectives, criteria, or steps in a work program. The criteria you use may be drawn from policies, control principles, regulations, accounting guidelines, or other requirements. Each criterion should be stated in positive and measurable terms.

**State criteria in positive and measurable terms.**

- **Finance policy requires transactions over $5,000 to be approved by the division manager.**
- **Accounts should be reconciled by an individual who does not have responsibility for transaction entry.**
- **Sensitive data should be sufficiently safeguarded to prevent unauthorized access, according to Company System Security Standards.**

Being absolutely clear about the criteria up front will sharpen your thinking, focus your testing, and help you later to determine the significance of results and the relationships among various points.

### 2. Write a Specific Condition.

The condition statement represents your finding or preliminary conclusion, and it is based on the evidence you gathered. The Comment Worksheet breaks the condition down into these two pieces—the conclusion and the evidence—to ensure that you have factual support for the point.

A statement of conclusion should be: ***factual, specific, objective, and written in one sentence.***

**33**

**A statement of condition should be factual, specific, objective, and written in one sentence.**

- **Transactions over $5,000 were not properly approved by the division manager.**
- **Account reconciliation was not separated from data entry.**
- **Access to data was not restricted to employees requiring it for their regular job duties.**

Being sure that the conclusion stands alone to express the key point will help you avoid writing weak sentences that may lead to misunderstanding or rewriting later in the process. Weak conclusions are **vague, cliché, or inconclusive.**

**Examples of Weak, Vague Condition Statements:**

- **Control weaknesses were noted.**
- **Procedures for reconciling accounts need to be improved.**
- **Exceptions were noted in the review of large transactions.**

Next, summarize the evidence from which you have drawn the conclusion. This section should not just duplicate detail already documented in your workpapers; it should highlight the key data that supports the point. It is likely that this evidence will be used in the final report, so you should keep it at a high level. Because you can easily cross-reference the detailed schedules or notes from the workpapers, it is not necessary here to go into many specifics.

The evidence selected for the Comment Worksheet will always be a summary. As you choose this information, consider what facts or examples best convey the significance or extent of the condition.

**Choose facts or examples that convey the significance or extent of the condition.**

- **Sixty percent of the 20 transactions reviewed were not authorized by the division manager.**
- **The clerk who enters accounting transactions also does the weekly reconciliation.**
- **A total of 120 users had access levels higher than those required by their job duties; another 20 users had terminated employment, but their access codes had not been deleted.**

If you are referencing a table or schedule, you should summarize the overall conclusion of that detail. For instance: ***"Credit limits had not been set for 15 percent of the customers reviewed, as shown in the attached schedule."***

Cross-referencing the associated detail also gives you an efficient method for sharing data with your client, as needed. If the detailed support is required for proof or corrective action, you can easily copy the workpaper page as a supplement to the Comment Worksheet.

### 3. Describe the Consequence from the Client's Point of View

In this section, you describe the business significance of the condition. Stating the consequence will help you determine the significance of the conclusion you have reached, based on the evidence you gathered. Think of the condition from the client's perspective, and consider questions such as the following.

**Consider the following questions to describe the consequence:**

- **So what?**
- **What has gone wrong or could go wrong as a result of the condition?**
- **What's the probable cost to the company?**
- **What's the risk, or extent of the exposure?**
- **How does this affect the client's business or operation?**

### 4. Analyze the Likely Cause

Your interviews, flow charts, or process reviews are most likely to help you identify probable causes of the issues you present. While you must be attentive to the specifics of the situation you are describing, you can also pinpoint problems by focusing on the most likely causes. Common causes include: *system design or use, process, policy, human error, resources, or circumstantial factors such as volume, staffing, or emergencies.*

Be specific and descriptive, not judgmental, as you identify causes. Also remember that in some cases it is not possible or practical to identify the root cause within the context of your fieldwork. If you feel that more time or work would be required to identify the cause, you should determine if this is cost-beneficial.

### 5. Make a Preliminary Recommendation

Focus here on a solution, not just a quick fix. The most valuable recommendations are aimed at preventing the condition from recurring, not just correcting the exceptions identified.

You will use your preliminary recommendation for discussion with management. As you reach consensus on this or another solution, you will document that agreement on the Comment Worksheet as "Management Action or Response."

# Common Questions about Comment Worksheets

### Do I Need to Complete All Five Cs All the Time?

Not necessarily. But, if you skip one of the 5 Cs, you should be able to explain why you did so. This means that you should always fully consider each of the 5 Cs.

For every comment, you should always document at least the following: *Condition, Consequence, and Corrective Action.* These components are necessary to develop a complete point, and they are the most likely elements to be carried forward to the final report. Perhaps the criterion is stated clearly in the work plan and does not need to be repeated in the comment; maybe the cause cannot be determined.

### What If I Don't Write Comment Worksheets Along the Way?

The quality and timeliness of the final report will suffer, and there may be a delay in getting agreement and action from management. Comment Worksheets keep you focused on the end result—your report—and they keep your clients informed and encourage prompt action. They are essential to an effective communication process.

### How Should I Document Positive Conditions?

You should document a condition for every step or procedure you perform, whether the result is positive or negative. Typically, only negative results need further development on the Comment Worksheet. It is important, though, to include your positive conclusions as you make presentations to management and as you consider the content of the final report. So don't overlook the importance and value of these positive results, and don't forget to document them.

## Write Comment Worksheets Throughout Your Project

Ongoing documentation and communication are essential to an effective and timely reporting process. Use of the Comment Worksheet and emphasis on the 5 Cs will enable you to assess the validity of your points, prepare convincing and constructive presentations to clients, and prepare the final report quickly. Your analytical skills will also be sharpened as you use the 5 Cs to develop complete and convincing points.

Remember that the 5 Cs and the Comment Worksheets are your tools for organizing your research, findings, data, and thoughts as you are completing a project. These are the templates you are filling in to develop the body of your report. While you may not use all the Comment Worksheets to write your final report, you will find that you will need all of them to determine what goes into your report. Therefore, you should be writing these worksheets throughout the course of your project.

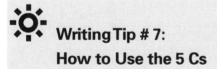 **Writing Tip # 7:**
**How to Use the 5 Cs**

Ongoing documentation and communication are essential to an effective and timely reporting process.

As you complete a project, take time out occasionally to write up your key results. This will enable you to compose a draft quickly at the end of the review.

## The Writing Process:
## How to Condense Detail into a Final Report

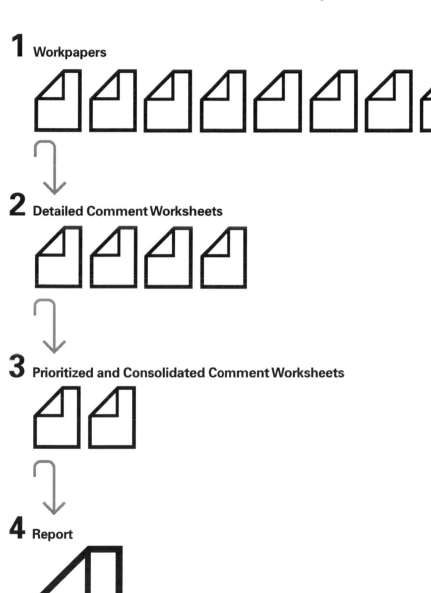

**1** Workpapers

**2** Detailed Comment Worksheets

**3** Prioritized and Consolidated Comment Worksheets

**4** Report

# Notes

CHAPTER 3

 **Organize the Report for Impact and Readability**

## Key Points

- Select the Appropriate Sections

- Structure the Report for Greatest Impact

- Layer the Report for Multiple Audiences

- Use Comment Worksheets to Compose the Body of the Report

- Format for Readability

- Write a Summary

- Use a Table of Contents for Longer Reports

- Decide on Organization and Format Before You Compose

# Notes

CHAPTER 3

# Organize the Report for Impact and Readability

## Select the Appropriate Sections

Once you complete your project work and have your key points documented on the Comment Worksheets, you are ready to structure and write the overall report. Audit, consultation, and review reports typically include some or all of the following sections.

**Sections of the Report**
Objective of the Project
Scope of Work Performed
Background Information
Overall Conclusion
Key Points or Results of the Project
Recommendations or Action Plans
Appendices or Attachments

In addition, it may be valuable to include certain identifying data that will provide control over the document and serve as archival information should the report need to be retained. Such data might include the items listed below.

**Identifying Data for a Report**
Title of the Report
Date of the Report
Time Period Covered by the Report
Names and Titles of Personnel Who Performed the Work
Names and Titles of Personnel Who Reviewed the Report
Identifying Number of the Report
Distribution List

As the author of the report, you should select and include the sections and the data that are necessary. You should base your decision on the following factors.

### Professional requirements:
Professional standards for Certified Public Accountants, Certified Internal Auditors, Certified Government Auditors, and others call for certain information to be included in written reports. Be sure you are familiar with your profession's standards and apply them in your reports.

### Company or departmental requirements:
To maintain consistency, your organization or your functional unit may have established standards or formats for you to follow in your reports.

### Size and scope of the distribution list:
Consider the individuals who are receiving your report. Identify and include the material that they need to fully understand and make use of your report.

### Coherence among the sections of the report:
Be sure the report is complete and logical.

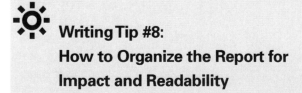

### Writing Tip #8:
### How to Organize the Report for Impact and Readability

You may structure your report according to:

- Conclusions
- Key Points or Results
- Recommendations or Action Plans
- Project Plan

# Structure the Report for Greatest Impact

Unless you are bound by certain company or professional requirements for report format, there are no rules dictating the order of the sections within your report. You should structure the report content so that your readers can easily and quickly find the information they most need and want.

You may choose one of four common report structures.

**Conclusions:**
This report structure puts the overall conclusions of the project in the first section, preferably on the first page. The overall conclusions are then followed by key points or recommendations supporting each of the conclusions. This design is effective for reports going to high-level management, reports that have a broad distribution list, or reports that focus on issues of immediate significance or high impact to the recipients.

**Key Points or Results:**
A report organized in this fashion lists the key findings of the project and discusses each issue one at a time. This order is often effective for the detailed section of a report that starts with overall conclusions, or it may be used as the body of the report when overall conclusions are not included. This arrangement allows the writer the flexibility to include as much or as little detail as needed to support each point. Writers should always present the key points in order of their significance.

**Recommendations or Action Plans:**
If your report is primarily a persuasive document, designed to initiate change or action, then this structure will be effective. The report will be organized according to the actions planned or recommended as a result of the project. You may order the recommendations according to the problems they will solve, their implementation date, or the unit or person responsible for the action.

**Project Plan:**

In this structure, the report follows a functional outline that is likely to follow the order in which the project was planned and completed. It starts with the project objective and scope, followed by findings or key points, and ends with an overall conclusion or recommendations. This structure is most appropriate for detailed technical reports directed to recipients who have a high degree of technical knowledge or interest in the subject matter.

## Writing Tip #9:
## Organize the Report for Impact and Readability

Always put the information of greatest significance up front in your report. Follow the lead of newspaper journalists. In their articles, the headline gets attention, and the first sentence tells the key point of the story. Busy readers browse through your report before diving into the detail. Don't run the risk of losing your audience before you get to your punch line.

## Layer the Report for Multiple Audiences

The wider your audience, the greater is the need for a layered report that will keep everyone's attention. Readers will have varying degrees of interest in, knowledge of, and responsibility for your topic. To avoid losing someone's interest, layer your report so that the most critical information comes first. Create your layers based on the interests of your highest-level readers first, and then follow in descending order. For instance, if the CEO of your organization is on your distribution list, you should start with the most high-level section (overall conclusions) and work your way down to detailed information such as scope of the project.

## Writing Tip #10:
## Organize the Report for Impact and Readability

Think of the report as a layer cake, with your highest-level readers' favorite flavors at the top. In that way, if a reader gets satisfied after the first layer or two, he or she is not missing the best parts.

Layering the report also gives you the flexibility of separating it into individual documents meeting the needs of different recipients. Line mangers, for example, may need detailed evidence from your project, while executive management may want only a short, crisp summary. Rather than issuing several versions of the same report, layering allows you to meet the needs of the highest level readers in the first page or two, which you can then separate as an executive summary.

For tips on how to write summaries, see *Tell It to the CEO: How to Write Compelling Executive Summaries and Briefings* by Angela J. Maniak.

# Use Comment Worksheets to Compose the Body

The issues you documented on the Comment Worksheets will form the basis for the body of the report. If you wrote these well, you will find composing to be quick and easy. To help select and organize the body of the report, try the following tips for using your Comment Worksheets.

### Compile Comment Worksheets According to the Objectives.

After you have finished your project, return to the statement of project objectives and organize the Comment Worksheets according to each one. This will help you state conclusions to your objectives and consider your key points in context.

### Select, Consolidate, and Prioritize.

All the issues you documented on Comment Worksheets may not make it into the report. Select those that are most relevant to the project objectives and most significant to the readers.

Once you have selected issues for inclusion, see if you can consolidate any of them. Are there repetitive themes, issues, impacts, or causes? If so, you may combine similar items. This will bring your issues to a higher level and also avoid redundancies.

Finally, remember to prioritize issues according to significance and list them accordingly in the report.

## Format for Readability

The look of your report is the first thing that will impress readers, either positively or negatively. Business professionals are inundated with reading material, and the documents that look easiest to read are often the ones that get read first. Therefore, make your document easy to read, no matter how short or long it is.

Begin with a distinctive cover sheet that identifies your work in a simple but informative way. List the title and date of the report, along with the name of your organization, firm, or department. Establish and use a consistent layout for the cover sheet for each report you or your organization writes so that recipients will recognize it immediately.

Give an **inviting look** to the body of the report by making it easy to follow and comfortable to digest. Avoid pages of straight type with little white space and few breaks, which look forbidding to many readers. Use headings that guide readers through the content and formatting that keeps their eyes moving along the pages. The following are simple yet effective formatting tools.

**Headings:**

Make headings descriptive and use an enlarged font or boldface type to make them stand out on the page. Readers browse through reports by reading headings, and you can convey information quickly by using headings effectively and generously.

**White Space:**

Small chunks of information are easiest for readers to understand and remember. Therefore, keep paragraphs short and use an extra line return between sections of the report. If you also use standard margins for the page layout you select, your report will have sufficient white space. You can create more by using other formatting tools such as lists or tables.

**Bulleted or Numbered Lists:**

You can frequently format detail or reduce repetition by organizing related items into bulleted or numbered lists. Remember to keep these brief.

**Tables or Charts:**

Numerical data is most readable when it is separated from the explanatory text. State your conclusion or key points in a sentence or two, and then offer detailed data in a simple table or chart.

**Writing Tip #11:**

**Organize the Report for Impact and Readability**

Formatting can make or break the success of your report. Be sure the font is legible (Times Roman 12 is standard for narrative reports), and use standard margins. Do not try to reduce the number of pages by minimizing the size of the font or the margins.

- Keep paragraphs short.
- Use descriptive headings.
- Arrange detail into lists, tables, or charts.

## Write a Summary

If your report is going to high-level management and it is more than three pages long, a summary is essential. Most business readers demand to know the key points of a report immediately and are intolerant of reports that do not get to the point quickly. Wrap up your key ideas in a few sentences or a few paragraphs and label them prominently on the first page.

## Use a Table of Contents for Longer Reports

A report of five or more pages should also contain a Table of Contents. If a reader wants to find a topic, he or she needs to know where to look. Make the Table of Contents correspond to the headings used in the body of the report so that readers can quickly find the link they need.

## Decide on Organization and Format Before Composing

To save time revising your report, decide on the organization, page layout, and formatting before you compose the draft. Once you make these selections, you can create templates or styles to use as you compose. You won't have to spend time thinking about formatting as you work on writing the body of the report.

Your report draft will display consistent formatting if you follow the choices you make in advance, and you will save many hours of editing time.

⊙ *Use the CD-Rom to see a sample of a formatted report.*

## Notes

## Notes

CHAPTER 4

 **Get to the Point!**

**Key Points**

⇄ Get Your Report Read and Understood

⇄ Start Each Section with the Key Point

⇄ Keep It Concrete

⇄ Convey Significance

⇄ Write in Simple Business Terms

## Notes

CHAPTER 4
# Get to the Point!

## Get Your Report Read and Understood

When your report lands on the desk of a business professional, it competes with scores of other documents for his or her attention. Will it get read quickly, or will it be put aside for another time? Will the recipient understand it at first reading, or will the report have to be studied so that the message becomes clear?

The opening line of every section you write is your best chance to get your report read immediately. Busy professionals are demanding of reports, and they are impatient with documents that do not make their point quickly and directly. Most business readers skim reports first, browsing at the headings and the key points to see if they are interested in reading further.

If you make the opening line of each section compact, direct, and interesting, you will create reports that get attention, invite your audience to read more, and generate a positive response. Here is how William Zinsser, a noted expert on writing, puts it:

*"The most important sentence in any article is the first one. If it doesn't induce the reader to proceed to the second sentence, your article is dead."*
From ***On Writing Well*** by William Zinsser

 **Writing Tip #12:**
**How to Write an Effective Opening Line**

- Get to the point.
- Make key points absolutely clear.
- Don't work up to the point with background information.

## Start Each Section with the Key Point

Give your readers what they want to know immediately. Most readers want to know your key point—your conclusion, finding, or recommendation—so put that in the first sentence of every section.

Writing a strong first sentence may not be as easy as it seems. In fact, this may be the most difficult sentence of every section to compose. Why? It requires clear focus, conclusive thinking, and descriptive language. One of the most common failures I see in reports is the use of weak first sentences.

Well-meaning writers often start a section with background information. This is a logical approach, starting at the beginning and moving forward toward factual evidence, conclusions, and recommendation. However, this is not an attention-getting approach, as it buries the key points readers most want to know. Such a deductive approach is what journalists call "burying the lead." Who wants to dig around in your report to find the good stuff? Most readers will walk away rather than bring out their shovels.

**Examples of Attention-Getting Opening Sentences:**

- **Commercial-loan documentation was incomplete.**
- **Operating expenses were understated by $1.2 million.**
- **Posting of transactions exceeded the one-day timeframe required by regulatory agencies.**
- **Access to confidential customer data was properly restricted to employees with a job responsibility requiring such access.**

## Writing Tip #13:
## How to Write an Effective Opening Line

### Follow the one-sentence rule:

Imagine that you are presenting your report to a major client who gives you only a moment of his or her time. You can offer only one sentence to convey each of your key points. What will that one sentence be? Make sure it is descriptive enough to stand alone.

## Keep It Concrete

Read the following sentences and consider what they all have in common.

- **The process is not functioning effectively.**
- **The following exceptions were noted.**
- **Security controls require improvement.**
- **Certain practices are informal and applied inconsistently.**
- **Controls over the receiving process are not adequate.**

What they all have in common is that they cannot stand alone. They don't say anything concrete; they simply offer generalizations. Such vague language is uninformative and likely to weaken the reader's attention. Generalizations also run the risk of becoming cliché. They are so generic that writers are likely to use them again and again. (They thrive in the copy-and-paste mode.) When they become reused, they become predictable and overdone. Overused language easily gets overlooked.

If you want to grab your readers' interest, you must use language that communicates a precise message. Keep your language concrete, descriptive, and factual.

**57**

## Writing Tip #14:
## How to Write an Effective Opening Line

To make your opening lines attention-getting, use concrete language that is:

- Factual
- Precise
- Descriptive

## Writing Tip #15:
## How to Write an Effective Opening Line

Avoid three common weaknesses in the opening line:

- Background information
- Generalizations
- Technical or unfamiliar language

## Convey Significance

Each opening line should interest readers sufficiently so that they are drawn to read more. Which of the following two sentences would keep you reading?

1. **Internal policies relating to pricing could be improved.**

2. **Pricing agreements totaling $1.5 million (25 percent of all open pricing agreements) did not show evidence of competitive bidding from suppliers.**

The first sentence gets to the point by describing an issue in one sentence, but it does not convey the significance of the issue. The second sentence not only gets to the point, it also conveys the size and scope of the issue. My vote goes to the second sentence. I am drawn into the issue from the start.

To convey significance in your opening lines, follow these guidelines:

1. **Be conclusive**.
2. **Convey the size or impact of the issue**.

**Be conclusive.**

Recipients of audit, financial, or review reports expect them to communicate conclusions, not just provide information. Therefore, give readers what they are looking for by making a conclusive statement—either positive or negative—in the opening line. Avoid neutral observations, inconclusive statements of fact, or background information.

### Example of a Neutral Observation:

### Accounts Receivable allows customers 30 days to pay invoices.

What conclusion is the reader to draw from this sentence? Is this a good situation or a bad one? Is this just background information, or is it a description of a problem? A reader's response to this sentence is likely to be "So?"

### Example of a Conclusive Opening Line:

### Accounts Receivable did not collect customer payments within 30 days, and did not charge interest or penalties for late payments.

**Convey the size or impact of the issue.**

Adding quantification to the opening line can convey the significance even more specifically.

**Example of an Opening Line with Quantification:**

**Invoices amounting to $2.2 million were paid on average 20 days past  the due date, with no interest or late fees charged.**

Notice also that the second half of the sentence ("with no interest or late fees charged") describes the impact, or consequence, of the past-due receipts. This is another effective way to convey the significance of an issue.

# Write in Simple Business Terms

If your readers do not speak the language you are using, they cannot understand your point. Your reports are likely to go to a diverse audience, so you have to consider the language of all your recipients. Let's start with an example of another opening line.

**Workprints and JMOS documents are not reviewed and approved.**

That may get the attention of someone intimately familiar with "JMOS documents," but it will leave other readers behind. Even spelling out the acronym may not solve the problem. Here is the revision.

**Workprints and JMOS (Job Management Operating System) documents are not reviewed and approved.**

The revised sentence still does not describe the issue in simple business terms. Even though readers may be able to understand the words used, they do not necessarily find them meaningful. To make the significance of the issue clear to a broad audience, the writer needs to substitute simpler business language.

**Example of an Opening Line in Simple Business Terms:**

**New-product pricing decisions are not reviewed and approved by the Director of Marketing.**

Start each section of your report with a conclusive, concrete sentence written in simple business terms. This will allow readers to skim your report and immediately learn your key points.

## Writing Tip #16:
## How to Write an Effective Opening Line

When you are describing technical or esoteric issues, consider your readers' proficiency in the language you are using. If some recipients are not familiar with the terminology, translate the terms into simpler business language.

## Exercise #2:
## Get to the Point!

**Describe the strengths and weaknesses of each of the four opening lines below.**

| Opening Line | Strengths | Weaknesses |
|---|---|---|
| 1. Company A owes Acme more than $52,000 in credits for last year, according to the terms of their agreement. | | |
| 2. The current version of Super Micr allows an individual to be signed on to the system via network access and VTAM simultaneously. | | |
| 3. There is potential for material and product mix-ups to occur in the plant. | | |
| 4. We examined a sample of 15 consumer mortgage folders to determine compliance with the advance disclosure provision of Regulation Z. | | |

⊙ *Use the CD-ROM to see suggested responses to this exercise.*

## Exercise #3:
## Get to the Point!

**Write an attention-getting opening line for the following paragraph.**

The Bidding Requirements and Procedures state that "the lowest bidder is to be awarded the contract unless the Contracting Office justifies and documents the reason for choosing a bidder whose quote is not the lowest." The Requirements further state that bidding exceptions are to be approved by the Director of Contracting. We noted three instances in which these requirements were not met:

| Vendor | Value | Date of Contract |
|--------|-------|------------------|
| Widget | $82,000 | 5-5-xx |
| Gadget | $51,500 | 5-1-xx |
| Acme | $99,000 | 6-3-xx |

⊙ *Use the CD-ROM to see suggested responses to this exercise.*

## Exercise #4:
## Get to the Point!

**Write a sentence in simple business terms as the opening for the following paragraph.**

Local Area Network (LAN) passwords for eleven user Ids have been set to "Never Expire." These user Ids have "Supervisor" access rights which grants them access to and control over the entire LAN system. Because the system has been set to "Never Expire" and the system does not require or prompt them to change their passwords, users may forget to or may delay changing their passwords. When passwords are not changed, there is a risk of a password becoming known and the risk of unauthorized access is thus greater.

⊙ *Use the CD-ROM to see suggested responses to this exercise.*

## Notes

CHAPTER 5

 # Sell Your Key Points: Make Your Report Persuasive

**Key Points**

- ⮂ Don't Write to Get Read;
  Write to Get Results

- ⮂ Offer Factual Evidence

- ⮂ Show Consequences from
  the Reader's Viewpoint

- ⮂ Describe or Quantify the
  Impact of Issues

- ⮂ Avoid Overstating or
  Understating the Significance

- ⮂ Confront Likely Objections

## Notes

CHAPTER 5

# Sell Your Key Points: Make Your Report Persuasive

## Don't Write to Get Read; Write to Get Results

How do you measure your return on the time you spend writing reports? Do you feel you get paid by the page? Do you seek feedback on how well recipients like your reports? If you want to make a mark through your report writing, neither of these is a true measure of your reports' success.

To get value from your reports, you should write not to get read, but to get results. A successful report leads to an active response from one or more recipients. When you write an audit, consulting, or review report, you do so because you want to initiate action in response to your results. The two types of action your report is likely to elicit are:

1. **Acceptance of your conclusions and results.**
2. **Implementation of your recommendations.**

If your intent is to get results or action in response to your report, then you need to be a persuasive writer. You are not just documenting results or communicating information. You are persuading your readers to take action.

> **Writing Tip #17:**
> **How to Sell Key Points**
>
> A persuasive writer needs to be not just clear, but also convincing.
> Make your reports persuasive by aiming for:
>
> - **Acceptance of your conclusions and results**
> - **Implementation of your recommendations**

## Offer Factual Evidence

Unsupported conclusions or generalizations are not persuasive. To convince
business professionals to take action as a result of your report, you need to
provide sufficient factual evidence to support your key points.

To illustrate persuasive techniques, I will use three sample condition statements.

### Examples of Condition Statements:

1. **Loan officers do not consistently obtain and file credit reports.**

2. **Some transactions were not properly categorized for accounting purposes.**

3. **Investment returns can be improved by reallocating cash balances.**

Each of these sentences begs for factual evidence to support it. Here are
revised versions, with factual support added.

**Examples of Condition Statements with Factual Evidence:**

1. **Loan officers did not obtain and file credit reports in 25 percent of the 50 commercial-loan files reviewed.**

2. **Purchases amounting to $1.6 million were not recorded in the quarter in which they were made.**

3. **Cash balances of $40 million can be invested in liquid instruments with a rate of return 1 percent higher than now achieved.**

While factual evidence is a persuasive strength, be careful not to overload the report with too much detail. Some writers go on and on with lists or tables of data. Although that data may be pertinent to the issue at hand, it belongs in the report only if it makes a persuasive point.

If you find yourself confronting lots of detail and not knowing whether it belongs in your report, consider a few criteria. First, does the evidence you are presenting directly support the conclusion or key point you are making? Second, does it show the significance of the issue? Finally, does the evidence point the way to a logical recommendation or corrective action? If your answer is yes to one or more of these questions, then the evidence is likely to add value to your report.

Remember that summarized or consolidated data makes a more persuasive case than a long list of detail. It is stronger to say: "Purchases amounting to $1.6 million were not recorded in the quarter in which they were made," rather than writing: "Seventy-three purchases were not recorded in the correct quarter. A list of those purchases follows."

## Show Consequences from the Reader's Viewpoint

Once the facts are established, you should address the question "So what?" The answer to this question will describe the consequence or the business impact. The consequence is a key persuasive element in report writing, as it addresses the most fundamental interest of the readers: "How does this affect me or my business?"

To write persuasive consequences, you need to describe these from the readers' point of view, not necessarily your own. Apply these three important techniques when you describe consequences.

1. **Avoid hypothetical or ambiguous consequences.**
2. **State the consequence in realistic and relevant terms.**
3. **Capitalize on actual consequences when you can.**

1. **Avoid hypothetical or ambiguous consequences.**

Let's consider again the first of the sample condition statements.

**Loan officers did not obtain and file credit reports in 25 percent of the 50 commercial-loan files reviewed.**

If writing from his or her own viewpoint, the author of the report might describe consequences in the following ambiguous terms.

**Examples of Consequences Written from the Writer's Viewpoint:**

- **This represents non-compliance with the company's credit policy.**
- **This could result in financial loss.**
- **As a result, credit files are incomplete and inconsistent.**
- **Credit files contain insufficient documentation for the loan officer's review.**

Such ambiguous language is likely to result in a "ho-hum" response from business readers. These consequences focus on documentation and compliance but not on business impact. To make the consequence more persuasive, the writer should describe the impact in business terms.

**Examples of Consequences Written from the Reader's Viewpoint:**

- **Without a review of credit reports, it is difficult to assess the customer's ability to repay the loan.**
- **Credit history is a key indicator of a customer's creditworthiness and should be used to determine appropriate loan amounts and repayment terms.**

2. **State the consequence in realistic and relevant terms.**

How do you turn a hypothetical statement into a realistic and relevant consequence? Let's use an example.

**Example of a Hypothetical Consequence:**

**Sharing of passwords could result in unauthorized access to the system.**

To make this statement more persuasive, consider answering the following questions:

1. **How many individuals share the same password?**
2. **Are there controls other than passwords that restrict access to the system?**
3. **What data is in the system?**
4. **What can someone do once he or she gains access to the system?**

Answers to the first two questions help determine whether the observation reflects a real problem and not just a hypothetical possibility.

**Example of a Realistic Consequence:**

**All system users—50 in total—share the same password, and the system does not require any identifying information other than the password.**

Answers to the second two questions help make the statement of consequence relevant by describing what users can do with their access.

**Example of a Relevant Consequence:**

**Users can add, delete, or change any text appearing on the company's web site. This may be done accidentally or with malicious intent.**

Combining the facts that answer the questions posed above results in a persuasive comment, showing a realistic and relevant consequence. See the following example.

**Example of a Consequence Written in Realistic and Relevant Terms:**

**All 50 system users share the same password, and the system does not require or track any other identifying information. Users can add, delete, or change any text appearing on the company's web site, either accidentally or with malicious intent.**

### 3. Capitalize on actual consequences when you can.

The samples I have given so far represent potential consequences. An even stronger persuasive device is the use of actual consequences. Using the last example, if the writer could identify how many times unauthorized access was achieved or attempted, this would add strong and credible evidence to the observation. Perhaps the writer could also identify instances in which unauthorized changes were actually made to the web site

Actual consequences are strong selling points. Use them when they are factual and relevant.

**Example of an Actual Consequence:**

**Testing identified 40 instances of unapproved postings to the company's web site over the past 30 days. Accountability could not be established because all 50 users with website access shared the same password.**

## WritingTip #18:
## How to Sell Key Points

Answer the **"So what?"** question by describing consequences from the reader's viewpoint.
- Avoid hypothetical or ambiguous consequences.
- State the consequence in realistic and relevant terms.
- Capitalize on actual consequences when you can.

# Describe or Quantify the Impact of Issues

When business readers read an observation, whether negative or positive, the first question they want answered is, **"How big is the problem or the profit?"** Persuasive reports that call for action must answer this question to be successful.

Most audit, consulting, and review reports include numbers, factual evidence, findings, and conclusions. Not all of them show how big these numbers and findings are to the organization or the individual recipients. Just because a report has numbers does not mean that the writer has quantified the impact of an issue.

To answer the question, **"How big is the problem or the profit?"** you must accomplish two things:

1. **Show the size or degree of the issue.**
2. **Put it in perspective.**

### 1. Show the size or degree of the issue.

I will illustrate the effect of quantifying the issue by using the three sample condition statements presented early in this chapter.

**Condition Statement #1:**

**Loan officers did not obtain and file credit reports in 25 percent of the 50 commercial-loan files reviewed.**

The above sentence itemizes the numbers of exceptions identified through testing, but it does not quantify the size of the issue. While it does provide factual evidence, it does not provide the context necessary to answer the question "How big is the problem?"

The following information provides context by expressing the value of the loans in question. This allows readers to grasp the scope of the exposure presented by the condition.

**Context for Condition #1:**

**In a sample of 50 commercial loans, 14 loans totaling $2.6 million were not supported by credit reports.**

Next, I will illustrate context for the remaining two samples.

**Condition Statement #2:**

**Purchases amounting to $1.6 million were not recorded in the quarter in which they were made.**

While this condition already indicates the dollar value, readers could better understand the size of the problem by knowing the percentage the amount represents.

**Context for Condition #2:**

**This represented 12 percent of the total purchasing amount for the previous quarter.**

Finally, let's consider the third example.

**Condition Statement #3:**

**Cash balances of $30 million can be invested in liquid instruments with a rate of return 1 percent higher than now achieved.**

This statement, which describes a possible increased profit, would benefit from quantification of the actual expected return.

**Context for Condition #3:**

**The result would be an increase of $30,000 annually in interest income.**

**2. Put it in perspective.**

The context provided in the samples above helps readers understand the size of the problem by putting the issues in financial perspective. An isolated number seldom tells the whole story. After all, $1 million can represent a lot of different things depending on its context. Does the $1 million represent an organization's total net income for the year, or does it represent 0.2 percent of revenue received?

Some techniques for putting issues in perspective include the following:

- **Quantify the value of the topic you are describing.**
- **Express the value as a percentage of the sample or the total.**
- **Offer a comparison to a standard, a benchmark, or past performance.**

Another way to put issues in perspective is to show the likelihood of a positive or negative impact. Again, let's consider a statement of consequence:

**Without a review of credit reports, it is difficult to assess the customer's ability to repay the loan.**

The potential consequence seems valid, but the reader may question how likely it is. How likely is it that the lack of a credit report leads to the nonpayment of a loan? The author of the report can address that question by considering the following:

- **Are there other reviews done or documents used besides credit reports to evaluate a customer's creditworthiness?**
- **Is there any historical correlation between credit reports and repayment?**

In a similar fashion, the writer of another report might address the likelihood of increasing the return on cash by considering additional questions:

- **Is the higher interest a fixed rate, and for how long is it available?**
- **Is the amount of available cash stable for the period proposed for the investment?**

Showing the likelihood of the consequence you are describing can be a strong selling point in your reports.

## Writing Tip #19:
## How to Sell Key Points

Remember to answer the question **"How big is the problem or the profit?"** Show the size or degree of the issue by putting it in context. Put it in **perspective** by indicating:

- The value or volume of the item you are describing.
- The value or volume as a percentage.
- A comparison to a standard or past performance.
- The likelihood of the consequence occurring.

# Avoid Overstating or Understating the Significance

Remember that the consequence is one of your strongest selling points, and be careful to avoid traps that often lead to disagreement or defensiveness from clients. Especially avoid overstating or understating the significance of the issue.

Overstating the significance is likely to cause defensiveness and may even lead the client to dismiss the credibility of your argument. Readers may perceive that the following language overstates the issues.

### Examples of Overstated Consequences:

- **This could cause financial loss.**
- **This compromises internal controls.**
- **Fraudulent transactions are likely.**
- **The system could fail.**
- **Severe penalties might be assessed.**

If you have ample evidence to support such statements, you might be able to justify use of such strong language. Otherwise, avoid overstating the issue by keeping the consequence in realistic and relevant terms.

On the other hand, understatements are likely to be dismissed by readers as insignificant. I recently read a report describing an incomplete disaster recovery plan. The writer described the consequence by saying, *"The company may not be able to resume operations quickly in the event of a disaster."*

This turned out to be the understatement of the year once I learned the details of the situation. I came to understand that the plan had no provisions for off-site processing, that backup files were made only once a week, and that the parts of the plan that were in existence had not been tested. It seemed to me that the consequence was a classic understatement in the light of such evidence. The writer rewrote the condition after considering these issues and presented the following statement in the final report.

**Example of a Realistic and Relevent Consequence:**

**The company would be likely to lose five days worth of data in the event of a system disruption, and it would take two or more days to locate and establish operations at an off-site processing facility. Critical functions such as invoicing, order fulfillment, and accounts receivable would be out of operation for up to a week.**

## Confront Likely Objections

If an opposing argument is strong, you may need to acknowledge and overcome that objection in your report. You may do this indirectly, by anticipating the readers' questions and providing answers in your narrative. You may also do this directly by building a balanced argument, recognizing the validity of readers' opinion, and realistically acknowledging alternatives.

### Use a balanced approach.

If a reader is opposed to your conclusions, findings, or recommendations, a critical or one-sided approach will cause further disagreement. Show balance and diplomacy by recognizing other legitimate points of view. For instance, if loan officers object to getting credit reports for existing customers each time they request new credit lines, the writer might recognize this in the report.

**Example of a Balanced Statement:**

**While an annual credit report can suffice for established customer relationships, loan officers should review a credit report for new customers each time they request an increased line of credit.**

Balance may also involve the recognition of positive accomplishments or efforts even when a problem still exists.

**Example of a Balanced Statement:**

**The Systems Department has drafted a disaster recovery plan but has not yet tested it.**

**Acknowledge alternatives.**

If you know of more than one way to address an issue you are presenting in a report, acknowledging the alternatives may help you sell your points. Rather than appearing to have tunnel vision, you can present yourself and your ideas as practical and accommodating.

## Writing Tip #20:
## How to Sell Key Points

Remain constructive in your tone when you are writing persuasively. Avoid overstating or understating the significance of issues. Confront likely objections by **using a balanced approach and acknowledging alternatives.**

# Four Steps to
# Building a Persuasive Case

1. What is the condition or issue?

2. What factual evidence can you provide?

3. So what? How does the issue affect the reader?

4. How big is the problem or the profit?

## Exercise #5:
## Sell Your Key Points

Take the condition described below and build a persuasive case by
answering the questions that follow.

1. What is the condition or issue?
   "Changes made to the payroll master file are not reviewed by
   someone independent of master-file updating and payroll
   processing."

2. What factual evidence can you provide?

3. So what? How does the issue affect the reader?

4. How big is the problem or the profit?

⊙ *Use the CD-ROM to see suggested responses to this exercise.*

# Exercise #6:
# Sell Your Key Points

**Assess the persuasive strengths and weaknesses of the following narrative.**

During our review of purchasing procedures, we noted the following:

1. Management has not established a formal purchasing policy for competitive bid documentation requirements. Our review of purchase orders indicated bidding may occur on some items, but formal competitive bid information is not documented.

2. Purchase orders for four of twenty transactions tested (valued at $7,500 in total) were issued after the order had been placed.

3. For six transactions where services were provided, purchase orders were used instead of service orders.

*Use the CD-ROM to see suggested responses to this exercise.*

## Notes

_____

_____

_____

_____

_____

_____

_____

_____

_____

_____

_____

_____

_____

_____

_____

_____

_____

_____

_____

_____

_____

_____

_____

_____

CHAPTER 6

 **Get Commitment to Key Points: Make Your Report Action-Oriented**

**Key Points**

⮂ Write Recommendations That Fix and Prevent Problems (Or Achieve and Maintain Profits)

⮂ Focus on the Cause

⮂ Write Measurable Recommendations

⮂ Write Practical Recommendations

⮂ Document Action Plans That Establish Accountability

⮂ Describe the Benefits of Recommendations or Action Plans

⮂ Focus on a Few Key Action Items

## Notes

CHAPTER 6

# Get Commitment to Key Points: Make Your Report Action-Oriented

## Write Recommendations That Fix and Prevent Problems (Or Achieve and Maintain Profits)

Your reports are likely to include recommendations or action plans to address the issues presented. The actions or solutions described are often the most valuable part of the report, as they lead to specific results or outcomes. If these actions lead to measurable improvement, their value is practical and measurable.

Reports may include preliminary recommendations that you offer readers for their consideration, or they may include action plans that have been discussed and agreed to by the affected parties. This chapter will discuss both alternatives.

Recommendations add value if they serve to fix and prevent problems, or if they serve to achieve and maintain profits. This means that recommendations must have both short- and long-term impact on the issue described. To write a recommendation, you should consider the following two questions:

1. **What will fix the problem (or achieve a profit) now?**
2. **What will prevent the problem from recurring (or maintain the profit in the future)?**

For example, consider the following two conditions:

1. **Contract files reviewed did not contain evidence of competitive bidding.**

2. **Investing cash balances into a money-market account will increase the interest earned.**

Recommendations to address the conditions might be:

1.  **Document the competitive bids obtained for the contracts awarded to establish complete files and compliance with company policy.**

2.  **Invest 80 percent of the current cash balance into a money-market fund.**

Those steps will address the current conditions, but they will do nothing to change future circumstances. What about contracts awarded in the future? What about maintaining or investing cash balances over time? The way to address these questions is to focus on the underlying cause.

## Focus on the Cause

To write a recommendation that will prevent the problem from recurring or maintain the profit in the future, you must focus on the underlying cause of the situation. Why did the contract files not include evidence of competitive bidding? Was it because there was no policy requiring this, or because no one reviewed the contracts independently to ensure compliance with the policy? Or was it because contracting personnel did not obtain competitive bids? Through your analysis and interviews, you can determine the cause of the condition and write a recommendation to address that cause.

**Examples of Recommendations Addressing the Cause:**

1.  **The Contracting Manager should review files before contracts are awarded to ensure competitive bidding has been considered and documented in accordance with company policy.**

2.  **Cash accounts should be set up to automatically sweep 80 percent of the balance into a money-market fund.**

**Writing Tip #21:**

**How to Get Commitment to Key Points**

Value-added recommendations focus on the underlying cause and should address two questions:

1. What will fix the problem (or achieve a profit) now?
2. What will prevent the problem from recurring (or maintain the profit in the future)?

**Avoid writing recommendations that repeat the condition.** These are not focused on the cause.

## Write Measurable Recommendations

To ensure successful implementation of recommendations, you must write them in measurable terms. Use language that someone other than yourself can use to measure implementation of the recommendation in the future. Avoid ambiguous and non-measurable terms such as the following:

### Examples of Ambiguous Recommendations:

- **Management should improve the reconciliation process.**
- **Consider revising the policy to require independent review.**
- **Record amounts properly.**
- **Receiving clerks should enter amounts received in a timely manner.**
- **The account should be reviewed periodically.**

How would someone measure implementation of the above recommendations? Words such as *"improve," "consider," "properly," "timely,"* and *"periodically"* are open to interpretation. It would be a matter of judgment to determine if the process were *"improved."* Instead of using ambiguous language, use terms that lend themselves to inspection or measurement.

**Examples of Measurable Recommendations:**

**The Finance Manager should reconcile the general-ledger account monthly, investigate and resolve differences, and retain documentation of the reconciliation for 12 months.**

**Receiving clerks should enter the volume of raw material received into the inventory system on the day of receipt.**

It is possible to determine implementation of the two recommendations above by inspecting evidence and measuring the timeliness. The writer has provided measurable recommendations.

 **Writing Tip #22:**
**How to Get Commitment to Key Points**

Value-added recommendations are written in measurable language. They use terms that lend themselves to **inspection or measurement.**

# Write Practical Recommendations

Remember that the value of your reports comes from having the recommendations **acted on promptly.** Therefore, recommendations should reflect:

1) **Available resources**
2) **Appropriate level of authority**

Reviewing preliminary recommendations with clients is essential to ensure that the proposed solution is feasible. Do the personnel, systems, expertise, or budget needed to fix the problem exist? If not, are they readily available? Also, when naming the person or function responsible for the recommendation, consider if that level has the authority not only to implement the action, but also to enforce it going forward.

# Document Action Plans That Establish Accountability

Even more valuable than a recommendation is an action plan that has been accepted by the parties who must implement the action. Action plans establish accountability and communicate the status of the plan to all recipients of the report. Complete action plans describe: 1) the action taken or to be taken, 2) the party or parties responsible, and 3) the targeted implementation date.

**Examples of Action Plans:**

**The Finance Manager will reconcile the general-ledger account monthly, investigate and resolve differences, and retain documentation of the reconciliation for 12 months. This process will begin January 31, 2xxx.**

**Effective February 1, 2xxx, the Receiving Manager will require receiving clerks to enter the volume of raw material received into the inventory system on the day of receipt. The manager will review the inventory report daily for compliance with the requirement.**

## Writing Tip #23:
## How to Get Commitment to Key Points

**Action plans** establish accountability. They include:
**What** action has been or will be taken?
**Who** will be responsible for the action?
**When** will the action be implemented?

# Describe the Benefits of Recommendations or Action Plans

If you have written the body of your report persuasively, describing consequences and quantifying impact, the benefit of the recommendation or action plan should be evident to your readers. If you have built a persuasive case, the solution will flow logically from the conditions, evidence, and consequences. The value of implementing the recommendation or action plan will be clear.

If there is any ambiguity about the value of the solution, you can address that by specifically describing the benefit of the action. For some cases, you may find it even more effective to include a cost-benefit discussion.

Often, you can incorporate the benefit right into the recommendation or action plan.

**Examples of Recommendations Including Benefits:**

**The Finance Manager should reconcile the general-ledger account monthly, investigate and resolve differences, and retain documentation of the reconciliation for 12 months. This**

**process will minimize delays in preparing quarterly financial statements, as differences will be identified and resolved each month.**

**Receiving clerks should enter the volume of raw material received into the inventory system on the day of receipt to ensure that inventory reports accurately reflect the amount of raw-material on hand for manufacturing.**

In more complex cases, you may want to include more information discussing the cost of the solution compared to the payback to be gained. Let's consider an example.

**Example of a Cost-Benefit Statement:**

**Recommendation:**
Automate the monthly account-reconciliation report, allowing managers to focus on resolving differences rather than producing reports

**Cost:**
Software purchases will cost approximately $25,000. Implementation can be done in-house at an estimated cost of $15,000. Users can learn the new software independently in less than 30 minutes, so training costs will be minimal. The new program can be running within 30 days.

**Payback:**
The software will allow the system to produce monthly discrepancy reports for management's review. This will eliminate the manual process, which now takes 25 users four hours apiece each month. The cost of implementing the new program will be recovered in less than a year, and the time-savings will be ongoing.

## Focus on a Few Key Action Items

To gain acceptance of recommendations, don't run the risk of overwhelming your readers with too many action items.

I have seen reports containing as many as 76 individual recommendations. I have read other reports that list 8 or 9 steps to address each item in the body of the report. Such long, detailed lists are hard to follow and may seem impossible to implement.

To facilitate a positive response to your report, consolidate action items wherever you can. Another approach is to group action items by category, including a manageable number of recommendations in each group. Always, of course, prioritize the action items so that readers know which steps are of most immediate significance.

## Notes

_____

_____

_____

_____

_____

_____

_____

_____

_____

_____

_____

_____

_____

_____

_____

_____

_____

_____

_____

_____

_____

_____

## Notes

CHAPTER 7

 **Say It Concisely**

**Key Points**

⇄  Say What You Mean in As Few
Words As Possible

⇄  Stay Clear of the Seven Deadly
Sins of Wordiness

⇄  Slash Sentences to Make
Every Word Count

⇄  Bias Your Writing Toward
the Active Voice

## Notes

# CHAPTER 7
# Say It Concisely

## Say What You Mean in As Few Words As Possible

"There are always too many words at first," asserts Jacques Barzun in his book, **Simple & Direct: A Rhetoric for Writers.** All good writers will come to the same conclusion when they review their own draft reports. It seems that wordiness comes naturally to most business writers, and it requires discipline to remove the extra words that get in the way of the message.

Why must writers work hard to make every word count? It is because business readers demand conciseness of the reports they read. With one document after another building up in the "To Be Read" file, business professionals are impatient with lengthy or verbose reports.

When I receive reports from clients, I perform triage immediately. I read the crisp and concise reports first. I do this because I get satisfaction from being able to complete my review of a document quickly. I put the more lengthy reports aside for another time, when I will have more energy and focus to do a thorough review. I ignore portions of some reports altogether. When I run into wordy, unclear, difficult-to-read passages, I skip to another section. I find myself resenting a writer who is taking too much of my time to get his or her point across.

The higher the level you are writing to, the greater is the demand for a concise style. The request I hear most often from high-level readers is for a one-page summary. The reason they ask for this is that the reports they get are too long. It is not necessarily that the reports have too much information; it is that they have too many words.

This chapter will show you how to say what you mean in as few words as possible.

## Writing Tip #24:
## How to Say It Concisely

Recognize that your first draft will not be as concise as it can be. Remember to review your work to remove unnecessary words and **make every word count.** Mark Twain once apologized to a friend for writing him a long letter. "I would have written you a shorter letter," he said, "but I didn't have the time."

## Stay Clear of the Seven Deadly Sins of Wordiness

Start by reviewing the following paragraphs to identify unnecessary words. Try to identify the seven deadly sins of wordiness by highlighting words you can delete or shorten.

**Example of Wordiness:**

Increased utilization of SAP would enhance controls and improve efficiencies.

During the review of the procurement process, we noted that key departmental personnel are not trained regularly on SAP system features. SAP provides certain functionalities that facilitate processes; however, we noted that certain users are not completely familiar with them. As a result, the system is not being used to its full advantage and some processes are still being performed manually by the users. Below are certain tools within SAP that are not being used that we identified during our review:

Request for Quotation (RFQ) to obtain prices from vendors.

Price analysis for comparison among vendors.

Third party performance metrics such as quality and service levels.

Utilization of the above tools would enhance controls and improve efficiencies. Management should conduct an analysis of the current tools that are available in the system. Additionally, it should be determined which of the current tools would provide the support functions that would be of assistance to users.

Here is the same paragraph, with the unnecessary and verbose words highlighted in boldface type.

**Symptoms of Wordiness Highlighted:**

**Increased utilization** of SAP would **enhance controls and improve efficiencies.**

**During the review of the procurement process, we noted that** key departmental personnel are not trained **regularly** on SAP system features. SAP provides **certain functionalities** that facilitate processes; however, **we noted that** certain users are not **completely** familiar with them. As a result, the system is not **being** used to its full advantage and some processes are still **being performed manually by the users.** Below are **certain** tools within SAP **that are not being used that we identified during our review:**

Request for Quotation (RFQ) **to obtain** prices from vendors.

Price analysis for comparison among vendors.

Third party **performance metrics such as** quality and service levels.

**Utilization** of the above tools would **enhance controls and improve efficiencies.** Management should **conduct an analysis** of the **current** tools **that are available in the system. Additionally, it should be determined** which of the **current** tools would **provide the support functions that would be of assistance** to users.

The highlighted words and phrases illustrate the following seven deadly sins of wordiness.

## The Seven Sins of Wordiness

1. Filler Phrases
2. Redundant Modifiers
3. Drawn-Out Verbs
4. Overstated Language
5. Empty Words
6. Passive Voice
7. Repetition

For each example of wordiness highlighted in the sample on the previous page, see if you can identify which of the seven sins it represents. Then turn to the next page to see my notes on the sample.

**Seven Sins of Wordiness Highlighted:**

---

④ ⑤
**Increased utilization** of SAP would **enhance controls and improve**

**efficiencies.**
①
**During the review of the procurement process, we noted that**
⑤
key departmental personnel are not trained **regularly** on SAP system
⑤
features. SAP provides **certain functionalities** that facilitate processes;
① ②
however, **we noted that** certain users are not **completely** familiar with
③
them. As a result, the system is not **being** used to its full advantage
③ ⑥
and some processes are still **being performed manually by the users.**
⑤ ②
Below are **certain** tools within SAP **that are not being used that we**
①
**identified during our review:**
⑦
Request for Quotation (RFQ) **to obtain** prices from vendors.

Price analysis for comparison among vendors.
④
Third party **performance metrics such as** quality and service levels.
④ ⑤
**Utilization** of the above tools would **enhance controls and**
③
**improve efficiencies.** Management should **conduct an analysis** of the
② ② ④ ①
**current** tools **that are available in the system. Additionally, it should**
⑤ ②
**be determined** which of the **current** tools would **provide the support**

**functions that would be of assistance** to users.

---

**The Seven Sins of Wordiness**
① Filler Phrases
② Redundant Modifiers
③ Drawn-Out Verbs
④ Overstated Language
⑤ Empty Words
⑥ Passive Voice
⑦ Repetition

Finally, look below for a concise revision of the sample. It shows what remains when the symptoms of wordiness are removed.

Even after removing the unnecessary and verbose words from the sample of wordiness, repetition still remains in the paragraphs. Deleting the repeated words and combining sentences results in the following concise paragraph.

**Example of a Concise Narrative**

Key personnel are not trained on SAP features that facilitate certain processes. As a result, the system is not used to its full advantage. The following SAP tools are available to replace manual processes:

- Request for Quotation from vendors
- Price analysis to compare vendors' quotes
- Third-party quality and service metrics

Management should determine which tools can support system users.

**Wordy v. Concise: Here Are the Numbers**

Original version: 164 words

Revised version: 62 words

**That is a 62% reduction in the length of the paragraphs!**

The following pages offer examples of the Seven Sins of Wordiness.

## Filler Phrases

Filler phrases take up space but add no meaning. You can delete them without changing the meaning of the sentence.

| Examples | Edited for Conciseness |
|---|---|
| ■ During our review<br><br>■ We noted that<br><br>■ It was noted<br><br>■ Review of . . . disclosed<br><br>■ It was determined that<br><br>■ This is to inform you that<br><br>■ There is potential that . . . could. . .<br><br>■ Develop and implement procedures to ensure that. . .<br><br>■ Our examination of . . . identified that . . .<br><br>■ It is understood that | *This column is blank because these phrases need no replacement. Just delete them.* |

# Redundant Modifiers

Redundant modifiers use unnecessary adjectives or adverbs or turn a simple adjective into a long phrase.

| Examples | Edited for Conciseness |
| --- | --- |
| ■ Current tools that are available in the system | ■ System tools |
| ■ Support functions that would be of assistance to users | ■ Support functions |
| ■ In the month of June | ■ In June |
| ■ On a daily basis | ■ Daily |
| ■ A wide variety of processing steps | ■ Many steps |
| ■ Charges that resulted from these types of transactions | ■ Charges resulting from these transactions |
| ■ Competent and responsible personnel from outside the organization | ■ Independent, experienced personnel |

## Drawn-Out Verbs

Drawn-out verbs turn simple action verbs into a noun phrase. Drawn-out verbs often contain a noun with the "tion" ending, and they always require a preposition.

| Examples | Edited for Conciseness |
|---|---|
| ■ Ensure the implementation of | ■ Implement |
| ■ Perform a verification of | ■ Verify |
| ■ Make an adjustment to | ■ Adjust |
| ■ Conduct an analysis of | ■ Analyze |
| ■ Do a review of | ■ Review |
| ■ Perform testing of | ■ Test |
| ■ Perform a reconciliation of | ■ Reconcile |

# Overstated Language

Overstated language uses longer, more complicated words where simpler, shorter words would suffice.

| Examples | Edited for Conciseness |
|---|---|
| ■ Utilization | ■ Use |
| ■ Additionally | ■ Also |
| ■ Due to the fact that | ■ Because |
| ■ In order to | ■ To |
| ■ Formal written procedures | ■ Written procedures |
| ■ By means of | ■ By; through |
| ■ At this point in time | ■ Now |
| ■ Sufficient to provide reasonable assurance that | ■ Sufficient |

**109**

## Empty Words

Empty words offer generalizations and do not stand alone.

| Examples | Edited for Conciseness |
|---|---|
| ▪ Enhance controls | |
| ▪ Improve efficiencies | |
| ▪ Used to its full advantage | |
| ▪ Appropriate | *This column is blank* |
| ▪ Improvement is needed | *because there are no* |
| ▪ It appears that | *direct substitutes for* |
| ▪ Areas requiring attention | *empty words. You should* |
| ▪ Ensure appropriateness | *use concrete and precise* |
| ▪ Some issues | *words instead of empty* |
| ▪ Generally adequate | *words.* |
| ▪ Inefficient | |
| ▪ Several | |

## Passive Voice

**Passive voice** uses a form of "to be" followed by the past participle and, usually, a prepositional phrase.

| Examples | Edited for Conciseness |
|---|---|
| ■ Procedures are being performed manually by users | ■ Users perform manual procedures |
| ■ The handling of collections is performed by the department | ■ The department handles collections |
| ■ Reconciliations of suspense accounts are performed by the supervisor | ■ The supervisor reconciles suspense accounts |
| ■ A management review will be completed of the account | ■ The manager will review the account |
| ■ Performance evaluations have been received by staff | ■ Staff have received performance evaluations |

## Repetition

**Repetition** results from using the same word within the sentence or repeating it from one sentence to the next.

| Examples | Edited for Conciseness |
|---|---|
| ■ Our test of expense reports revealed that expense reports contained exceptions. | ■ Expense reports contained exceptions. |
| ■ Supporting documentation was not attached to support expenses | ■ Supporting documentation was not attached. |
| ■ Procedures are in place to prioritize program changes and properly monitor program changes. | ■ Procedures are in place to prioritize and monitor program changes. |

## Writing Tip #25: How to Say It Concisely

Hunt for and remove the seven deadly sins of wordiness from your writing.

1. **Filler Phrases**
2. **Redundant Modifiers**
3. **Drawn-Out Verbs**
4. **Overstated Language**
5. **Empty Words**
6. **Passive Voice**
7. **Repetition**

# Slash Sentences to Make Every Word Count

To achieve conciseness in your own writing, review your draft with the goal of making every word count. In a concise sentence, every word adds meaning. You cannot remove words from a concise sentence without changing the meaning. Review your sentences, hunting for the seven deadly sins of wordiness.

To give you some practice before you move on to your own writing, edit the following example for conciseness.

## Exercise #7:
## How to Say It Concisely

**Make the following sentences as concise as you can without changing the meaning.**

1.  We recommend that these situations be reviewed by the Director of Contracting to ensure the decisions made by the Contracting Supervisor were appropriate. We further recommend that the Contracting Supervisor be reminded of the importance of documenting and obtaining proper approval anytime the lowest bid is not accepted on a major contract. Proper documentation and approval to support exception bids helps to ensure that the Company is receiving quality service at a competitive price.

2.  During our review of forty loan files we noted five instances where the required monitoring information was not collected and maintained. In four of the five situations noted, the application had been received by mail and the information had not been completed by the client. We recommend that all loan officers be reminded of their responsibility to collect and maintain the required government monitoring information.

3.  The Division is responsible for uploading and downloading mainframe data on a daily basis. There are four files that are uploaded and downloaded which have been placed under the mainframe-based Resource Access Control Facility (RACF) to restrict access to the data. The file downloaded each morning contains production data that should not be changed or altered; however, several individuals within the Division have been granted update access to the file.

⊙ *Use the CD-ROM to see suggested responses to this exercise.*

# Bias Your Writing Toward the Active Voice

The passive voice, which I have listed as a cause of wordiness, gets a lot of publicity in books and classes on writing. Most writing experts describe it as an evil element in business writing, so it is important that you understand more about it. My opinion is not that you have to ban the passive voice from your writing, but rather that you have to manage it effectively.

What is wrong with the passive voice? Frequently, the writer leaves out the "by whom" part of the sentence, making the message ambiguous. Consider the following sentences.

### Examples of the Passive Voice:

**A new procedure will be developed.**
**Data was entered into the system.**
**An independent review should be done.**

None of these sentences makes clear who is doing the action. When specificity or accountability is important, these passive sentences can cause confusion or misinterpretation.

Of course, the writer could solve the problem by adding a prepositional phrase. For instance: *"A new procedure will be developed by the Sales Manager."* However, this style of writing in the passive voice is wordy. Revising the sentence to the active would make it shorter: *"The Sales Manager will develop a new procedure."*

When is it appropriate to use the passive voice? Reserve the passive voice for those instances where you cannot identify the subject because it is not known, or where you choose not to identify the subject because it is not important.

## Writing Tip #26:
## How to Say It Concisely

Prefer the active voice. Write sentences with a subject that acts, using the "Who Does (or Did) What?" structure. For example:

- **Customer service representatives have authority to give refunds.**
- **The Finance Manager will approve the new policy.**
- **The supervisor reconciles the account weekly.**
- **Users do not have unique passwords.**

## Writing Tip #27:
## How to Say It Concisely

Learn to recognize the **passive voice.** It includes a form of *"to be"* followed by the *past participle* of the verb. For example:

- **Refunds *are granted* by the customer service representatives.**
- **The new policy *will be approved.***
- **The account *is reconciled* weekly.**
- **One system password *was shared* by all users.**

Limit the passive voice to situations in which you cannot or do not want to identify the subject of the action.

## Exercise #8:
## How to Say It Concisely

**In the following passage, identify each use of the passive voice. Then change the passive voice to the active voice. You may need to add a subject in some cases.**

> Verifications of signatures for compliance with official check signing guidelines were not being performed by the Operations Department. We noted several instances in which checks had not been signed by the two required individuals, and approvals for these exceptions to policy were not obtained and documented. Procedures should be implemented to identify checks lacking the necessary signatures. Proper authorizations should be obtained in a timely manner.

⊙ *Use the CD-ROM to see suggested responses to this exercise.*

## Notes

CHAPTER 8

 **Fine-Tune Your Writing: Do an Effective Self-Review**

**Key Points**

- Let Your First Draft Cool

- Check the Clarity and Completeness of Your Message

- Don't Let Mistakes Slip By: Perform a Self-Edit

- Beware Automated Editing Tools

- Get the Most Out of Useful Writing Tools

## Notes

CHAPTER 8

# Fine-Tune Your Writing: Do an Effective Self-Review

## Let Your First Draft Cool

No one writes a perfect first draft. Self-review is essential to producing a clear, complete, and correct report. Unfortunately, most writers find it difficult to be objective about their own writing. It seems easier to find the mistakes in someone else's writing than your own. Nevertheless, you are the person most equipped to edit your own work. After all, you are person who best knows what you want to say.

To do a thorough and objective self-review, you need to put your report aside for a while after you finish composing it. This will give you time to cool off from the heat of the writing process, put your mind on other things, and come back to the report with a fresh and objective perspective.

The cooling-off period should be at least overnight and preferably longer. You need to start writing well before the deadline for your report, as you need to build in a few days for cooling-off and editing.

## Check the Clarity and Completeness of Your Message

Your first reading of your report should be for clarity and completeness only. Do not make any detailed edits in this first reading. Instead, put yourself in the position of one of your readers.

For my first self-review, I like to print a copy of my report and sit at my desk, imagining that I am the client who has just received the report. I read first for the message: Are the key points clear? Is the report complete? Does the report flow easily? If I catch a typo or grammatical mistake, I mark it immediately, but my focus is on the content of the report. I take notes in the margins or on a separate sheet of paper.

### Questions to Consider for Your First Self-Review:

- Is the purpose of the report immediately clear?
- Is it quick and easy to find the key points in the report?
- Does the report get to the point by offering concrete opening lines?
- Is the factual evidence sufficient to support the key points?
- Does the report build a persuasive case?
- Are recommendations written in measurable terms?
- Do action plans establish accountability?
- Are the relevant sections included in the report?

For a report that has multiple audiences, I sometimes do this review more than once, each time considering a particular reader on my distribution list. After completing the self-review, I make changes and do another printout so that I can edit the draft in detail.

 **Writing Tip #28:**
## How to Do Effective Self-Review

Put your draft report aside after you finish composing so that you can clear your mind before you start reviewing it. Read first as a recipient of the report, focusing on the clarity and completeness of the content.

# Don't Let Mistakes Slip By: Perform a Self-Edit

My most embarrassing moment as a writing consultant occurred when I discovered that a client had received a report from me with a typo on the first page. Mistakes that go undetected and undisturbed in the review process seem to jump right off the page the minute they get into the hands of a client.

As an accounting, audit, or financial professional, your work is held up to high standards. Your reports must be absolutely accurate and grammatically correct. To achieve this goal, you must edit your reports for:

- **Accuracy**
- **Consistency**
- **Correctness**
- **Readability**

### Accuracy
Facts, data, and statistics you include in your reports must, of course, be accurate. Your proofreading, therefore, should include checking your facts against source documents.

### Consistency
Formatting and stylistic conventions should be consistent throughout the report. Check to see that the font, the margins, the spacing, and the style of headings are the same on every page. Also, any names or titles (of people, places, or things) should be presented consistently throughout. Abbreviations or symbols should also be consistent.

If you write the same type of report regularly, you may want to create a template or style guide to help you remain consistent.

### Correctness
Grammar, punctuation, and spelling must be correct. Careful proofreading will be necessary to ensure you catch and correct any mistakes. If your grammar skills are rusty, use reference books and editing tools to help you.

### Readability

Your proofreading gives you a final chance to make your report concise. Watch for the seven deadly sins of wordiness as you review, and take this opportunity to streamline your message further for your readers.

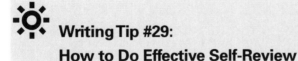

## Writing Tip #29:
## How to Do Effective Self-Review

Print a copy of your report and proofread carefully. Edit for:

- **Accuracy**
- **Consistency**
- **Correctness**
- **Readability**

# Beware Automated Editing Tools

You should certainly use the automated editing tools that are available to you, but remember to do so with caution. None of these tools is a substitute for your own careful proofreading. Spell check, for instance, is a godsend, catching typos writers easily overlook, but there are many mistakes and misspellings that will pass right through spell check undetected. Only you can find these hidden flaws.

I heartily endorse the use of spell check and, in fact, recommend that you spell check every single document you create. I suggest, though, that you print and proofread hard copy as if you had not run spell check. Be diligent and thorough. Don't skim; read every word. You may want to try an alternative practice— proofreading first, before you run spell check. Let spell check catch anything you might have missed, rather than vice versa. I established this practice myself after I found myself getting complacent in my proofreading. I often figured, "I've already spell checked. I can just skim through this document." That is when mistakes started getting through.

**Oops! These sentences went right through spell check:**

1. **The accounting manger adjusted the account balances.**
2. **No smoking aloud in the auditorium.**
3. **The account valance was overstated.**
4. **The revised policy has now been implemented.**

Explanation:
1. The word "manger" should be "manager."
2. The word "aloud" should be "allowed."
3. The word "valance" should be "balance."
4. The word "now" should be "not." The writer meant to say that "the policy has not been implemented."

Grammar check is another matter. It will highlight suspicious grammatical constructions, but it is up to you to figure out whether or not a change is necessary. My experience is that grammar check is right less than 50 percent of the time, and so I use other resources to check grammar.

**Oops! These sentences went right through grammar check:**

1. **We identified numerous errors in our review of expense reports.**
2. **No smoking beverages or food in the conference room.**
3. **The supervisor agreed to review the policy in a meeting with her boss.**

Explanation:
1. "In our review of expense reports" is a misplaced modifier. The sentence should read: "In our review of expense accounts, we identified numerous errors."
2. Commas are missing, leading to the phrase "smoking beverages." The sentence should read: "No smoking, beverages, or food in the conference room."

3. The phrase "in a meeting with her boss" may be misplaced and causes confusion. Did the supervisor agree to review the policy with her boss, or did she agree to review the policy, as a result of a meeting she had with her boss?

**Writing Tip #30:**
**How to Do Effective Self-Review**

Follow these tips for proofreading your report:

■ Work off of a hard copy. (Print it on scrap paper.)
■ Read word by word, focusing on correct spelling and consistency of words.
■ Read sentence by sentence, focusing on punctuation, grammar, and completeness.
■ Read one paragraph at a time, going backwards from the end of the report.
■ Review for consistency of headings, abbreviations, capitalization, numbers, and fonts.

## Get the Most Out of Useful Writing Tools

The most effective tools for self-editing are style guides and grammar reference books. Whether these are in automated or hard-copy form, they provide guidelines for establishing stylistic consistency and grammatical correctness.

**Style guides** outline conventions for items such as capitalization, spelling of names and titles, presentation of numbers, and sometimes formatting. A style guide is most effective when it is specific to a group or organization. Your company may have a corporate style guide indicating how to present product names and other information specific to the organization. Your business unit or department may have a style guide unique to the types of reports you write.

**Grammar books** are best used as reference material. When you are uncertain of your punctuation, sentence structure, or capitalization, you can find the answer in a good grammar reference. Hundreds of such books are in print, so how do you select one? The best grammar reference is one you are comfortable using.

A book on the shelf does you no good. If you have a favorite grammar book you have been keeping since high school or college, start with that. An older book might not include all current linguistic challenges, but most of its content will still be relevant.

If you are looking for a new grammar book, start in the reference section of a bookstore so that you can look over a few publications. Start by looking at the layout. Are sections clearly labeled with descriptive headings so that you can easily locate what you need?

Next, check the completeness and usefulness by going to the alphabetical index at the back of the book. Choose a topic you are interested in. Let's say you are confused about capitalizing titles and names of departments. Look up the page reference for "capitalization" and turn to that section. Read through the section to see if you can find a clear explanation that answers your question. Try this with two or three different topics. I have found this "hands-on use" test to be the best determinant of whether a reference book will work for me.

## The Final Step

When you have finished your self-review (and possibly peer- and supervisory-review), you can confidently issue your report to your client. You will deliver a clear, concise, useful report that will demonstrate the value of your work.

## Notes

# Writing High-Impact Reports:
Proven Practices for Auditors and Accountants

## Personal Action Plan

List techniques you will apply in writing your reports. Reference the page or chapter number so that you can find resources easily.

_____

_____

_____

_____

_____

_____

_____

_____

_____

_____

_____

_____

_____

_____

_____

_____

_____

## Personal Action Plan

_____

_____

_____

_____

_____

_____

_____

_____

_____

_____

_____

_____

_____

_____

_____

_____

_____

_____

_____

_____

_____

# ABOUT THE AUTHOR

**Angela J. Maniak** is a leading expert in helping business and government professionals communicate clearly, quickly, and convincingly. Since 1986, Angela has consulted to over 100 organizations and trained thousands of professionals to gain attention, acceptance, and action through their reports and presentations. She has taught throughout the U.S. and in Africa, Asia, Canada, Europe, Mexico, and South America.

Angela's other published books include:

- ***Tell It to the CEO:*** How to Write Compelling Executive Summaries and Briefings
- ***To Revise or Not to Revise:*** The Essential Guide to Reviewing Somebody Else's Writing
- ***Report Writing for Internal Auditors***

Angela has pioneered scores of practical approaches to solving on-the-job writing problems. She has helped her clients slash their writing and review time by 50% or more, publish documents on time and at a low cost, and design documents that executives actually read and remember! Angela's approach is practical and to-the-point. Angela doesn't just advise you on what to do — she shows you precisely how to do it.

**www.angelamaniak.com**

# Skill-Builders Press Order Form

SAN: 256-2618

**Ship to:**

Name: _____ Title: _____

Organization: _____

Shipping Address: _____

City: _____ State/Province: _____ Zip/Mail Code: _____

Country: _____

Phone: _____ Fax: _____

E-mail: _____

**Take a discount on quantity purchases! You can mix and match titles.**
10-25 copies: 10% discount
26-50 copies: 15% discount
50 + copies: 25% discount

| Title | Quantity | Price Ea. | Discount | Total |
|---|---|---|---|---|
| **Writing High-Impact Reports:** Proven Practices for Auditors and Accountants | | $59.00 | | |
| **Tell It to the CEO:** How to Write Compelling Executive Summaries and Briefings | | $59.00 | | |
| **To Revise or Not to Revise:** The Essential Guide to Reviewing Somebody Else's Writing | | $49.00 | | |

**Please see reverse to continue with your order....**

Please add shipping charge of 10% of order price:_____

(Customers outside the U.S., add 20%)

Total submitted: $_____

**All payments due in U.S. dollars.**

☐ Check enclosed, made payable to Skill-Builders Press

☐ Charge credit card:

Card #_____ Expiration Date_____

Name on Card_____

Type of Card    ☐ Visa         ☐ MasterCard         ☐ American Express

## Order Now!

**Call:**   207-338-0108

**Fax:**   207-338-0662

**Mail:**   Angela Maniak

Skill-Builders Press

191 Prescott Hill Road

Northport, ME 04849, USA

## Want to learn more?

Workshops and consultations are also available. For more information, or to order workbooks, please contact:

Angela J. Maniak

207-338-0108

www.angelamaniak.com